Straight Talk About...
RACISM and PREJUDICE

Marguerite Rodger and
Jessie Rodger

Crabtree Publishing Company
www.crabtreebooks.com

Straight
Talk About...

Developed and produced by: Plan B Book Packagers

Editorial director: Ellen Rodger

Art director: Rosie Gowsell-Pattison

Fictional Introductions: Rachel Eagen

Editor: Molly Aloian

Project coordinator: Kathy Middleton

Production coordinator: Margaret Amy Salter

Prepress technician: Margaret Amy Salter

Consultant: Susan Rodger, PhD., C. Psych., Psychologist and Professor Faculty of Education, The University of Western Ontario

Photographs:
Title page: Soubrette/iStockPhtoto.com; p. 4: hartcreations/iStockPhoto.com; p. 6: Ansar80/ Shutterstock Inc.; p. 8: Käfer Photo/ Shutterstock Inc.; p. 9: Mathagraphics/Shutterstock Inc.; p. 11: Joe Pitz/ Shutterstock Inc.; p. 12: Narvikk/iStockPhoto.com; p. 14: Ventura/Shutterstock Inc.; p. 15: Jason Mintzer/ Shutterstock Inc.; p. 16: Hart Creations/ iStockPhoto.com; p. 17: Sergey Prygov/Shutterstock Inc.; p. 18: Ewen Cameron/Shutterstock Inc.; p. 19: Brasil2 /iStockPhoto.com; p. 20: Elke Dennis/ Shutterstock Inc.; p. 22: Kharidehal Abhirama Ashwin/ Shutterstock Inc.; p. 23: Marcel Jancovic/Shutterstock Inc.; p. 24: AndreasReh/iStockPhoto.com; p. 25: Kharidehal Abhirama Ashwin/Shutterstock Inc.; p. 26: CURA Photography/Shutterstock Inc.; p. 27: Travel Photographer/iStockPhoto.com; p. 28: Inginsh/ Shutterstock Inc.; p. 29: Helder Almeida/Shutterstock Inc.; p. 32: Tyler Olson/Shutterstock Inc.; p. 34: Mona Makela/Shutterstock Inc.; p. 35: Haak78/Shutterstock Inc.; p. 36: F. Carucci/Shutterstock Inc.; p. 38: ZouZou/ Shutterstock Inc.; p. 40: Golden Pixels LLC/Shutterstock Inc.; p. 41: Pix Deluxe/iStockPhoto.com

Library and Archives Canada Cataloguing in Publication

Rodger, Marguerite
      Racism and prejudice / Marguerite Rodger and Jessie Rodger.

(Straight talk about--)
Includes index.
Issued also in an electronic format.
ISBN 978-0-7787-2129-1 (bound).--ISBN 978-0-7787-2136-9 (pbk.)

      1. Racism--Juvenile literature. 2. Prejudices--Juvenile literature. I. Rodger, Jessie II. Title. III. Series: Straight talk about-- (St. Catharines, Ont.)

HT1521.R62 2010   j305.8   C2010-903220-9

Library of Congress Cataloging-in-Publication Data

Rodger, Marguerite.
  Racism and prejudice / Marguerite Rodger and Jessie Rodger.
    p. cm. -- (Straight talk about--)
  Includes index.
  ISBN 978-0-7787-2136-9 (pbk. : alk. paper) --
  ISBN 978-0-7787-2129-1 (reinforced library binding : alk. paper)
  -- ISBN 978-1-4271-9542-5 (electronic (pdf))
  1. Racism--Juvenile literature. 2. Prejudices--Juvenile literature.
  I. Rodger, Jessie. II. Title. III. Series.

  HT1521.R627 2011
  305.8--dc22
                                                        2010019132

Crabtree Publishing Company

www.crabtreebooks.com   1-800-387-7650

Printed in China/082010/AP20100512

Published in Canada
Crabtree Publishing
616 Welland Ave.
St. Catharines, ON
L2M 5V6

Published in the United States
Crabtree Publishing
PMB 59051
350 Fifth Avenue, 59th Floor
New York, NY 10118

Published in the United Kingdom
Crabtree Publishing
Maritime House
Basin Road North, Hove
BN41 1WR

Published in Australia
Crabtree Publishing
386 Mt. Alexander Rd.
Ascot Vale (Melbourne)
VIC 3032

CONTENTS

The smell of chlorine hit Mark's nostrils as he walked into the changeroom. He could hear laughing and splashing on the other side of the door. Outside, a lifeguard blew a whistle. He changed into his swimming trunks and smiled to himself. Summer vacation. Two months of staying up late. It meant baseball and freedom. He couldn't wait. Mark walked out onto the sun-drenched deck. Des and Jorge were taking turns cannonballing water onto the sunbathers. Mark threw his towel onto the fence and walked over to his friends.

"Hey, guys. What's up?"

Jorge smiled. "What took you so long? We've been here for hours."

"It's my fault my sister borrowed my bike? I had to wait for her to come home." Mark dipped a toe into the water. It was cool. He took a deep breath and jumped in. He swam up beside Jorge and Des.

That's when he heard it. A sneering voice and the sound of laughter. He looked around. Some older kids were huddled at the edge of the pool, looking in his direction.

He heard it again. "Wash yourself."

"Those guys are looking at you." Des looked at the older boys. "Man, I don't want to fight."

One of the older boys pointed at Mark and pinched his nose with his fingers. Another boy waved his hand over his nose. "Dirty!" he shouted.

Mark's cheeks burned. He looked down at his skin, then up at the other swimmers. It felt like the whole world was looking at him. Some kids smiled, trying not to laugh. Others just stared. This wasn't the way summer was supposed to start. Sometimes Mark wished he could be invisible.

Introduction
Racism Hurts

Mark is struggling against the everyday injustices of racism and prejudice. He isn't alone. Racism and prejudice are major issues in society. Racism is the belief that people of different ethnic backgrounds are unequal. Prejudice is the unfair and unequal treatment of people because of a number of things, including their race, culture, religion, **sexual orientation**, or abilities. Racism and prejudice are never just.

In this book, you will learn some of the different ways that racism and prejudice hurt. You will learn how to deal with racism and prejudice, how it touches all of our lives, and why it is important to get help if you are being targeted.

"I wouldn't mind if people ask me why I wear **hijab**
I would tell them why. It's just that they assume I
was forced to do this against my will. It is my
choice, and I thought very hard about it because
it would be easier not to. It makes me an easier
target for hatred and ridicule."
Najima, aged 16.

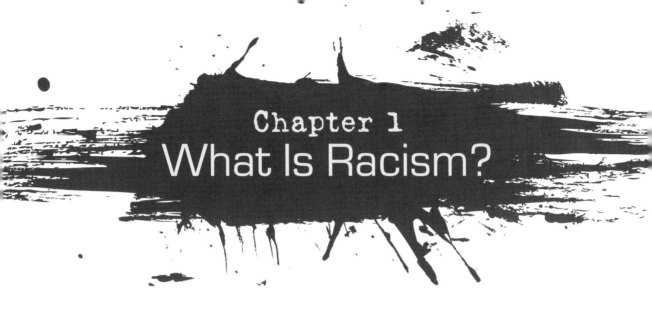

Chapter 1
What Is Racism?

Racism is the belief that one race, or group of people, is **superior** to another. Racism is hate. It is an intense dislike of another person for **superficial** reasons, such as the color of their skin, their culture, or where they were born.

Learned and Unlearned

Racist beliefs are learned opinions rather than scientific facts. Young people may hear racist thoughts and ideas from friends, family members, and even authority figures, such as teachers, police, or even church leaders. It may be difficult to separate fact from fiction, especially if someone you trust is the one making racist comments. By understanding what racism is and how to deal with it, you can learn to form your own **unbiased** opinions. You can also do your part to change society from one that is suspicious of and rejects or barely **tolerates** people of different skin colors, religions, and ways of life, to a society that accepts, lives peacefully with, and even embraces difference.

What Does It Look Like?

You must be able to identify racism in order to stop it. Racist beliefs often lead to **discrimination**, as well as violent acts including **hate crimes**. So, what does racism look like? Imagine that a new student comes to your school. The student approaches a group of kids in the schoolyard, looking for some company, only to be told that she cannot join in on the fun. The reason? The student's eyes are green instead of blue.

How would you feel if you were that green-eyed kid? Why would anyone reject you or treat you differently because of the color of your eyes? It seems silly and wrong, doesn't it? The group of students in the schoolyard may not realize that their actions are **offensive**. But this sort of behavior happens every day. Why is it any different to be discriminated against if your eyes are green than if your skin color is black or brown?

People are not born racist. So, where do people learn how to be racist? Quite often, racism is born from fear. Fear of others can be passed on from generation to generation. Some children learn how to be racist from the adults in their lives.

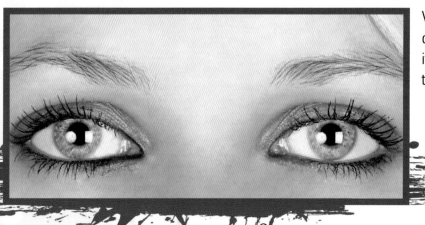

Why should skin color matter? Is it any different than eye color?

What Is Race?

When we talk about racism we may ask ourselves, what is race? Race describes the division of humans into different groups based on physical appearance, such as skin color, hair texture, or eye shape. This concept is something that human beings created. Race is not a fact of nature or science. In fact, scientists have proven that 99.9 percent of humans are **genetically** identical. People of all colors, cultures, and backgrounds are more **biologically** alike than they are different, even if our skin color and eye shape are different.

Unfortunately, racism has played a big part in shaping our history. To end racism we have to understand the incredible power it has held for generations, how devastating it has been, and how many people it has touched.

Human Difference

Every human is one of a kind. We all have different physical features such as skin color, eye color, weight, and height. We also have different **cultural** backgrounds, beliefs, and abilities. These differences make our world richer, but sometimes difference makes people fearful. That fear makes those who are different within a group targets for hatred and prejudice.

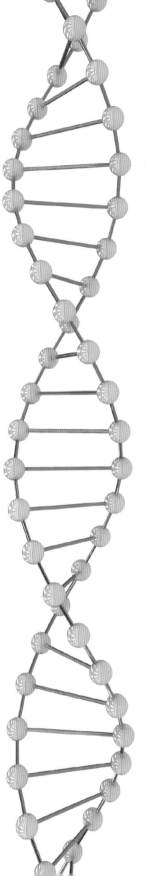

Our DNA, or hereditary material, cannot identify race.

R U Prejudiced?

What is prejudiced behavior? Imagine you are at school when your teacher announces that a new student is joining the class. Your teacher tells you this new student has moved from a town you have never been to. You have heard rumors that most people that come from that town are rude and snobby. Automatically, you assume that this new student will be rude and snobby, and you decide that you do not like him or her, even before you have met.

How would you feel if the roles were reversed? How would it feel to move to a new school, knowing that everyone had decided whether they liked you or not before you even got to speak to them or know them?

What Is Prejudice?

Prejudice is making a decision and forming an opinion about someone (or a group) you know nothing about. Some people have prejudiced feelings about a person or group of people based on their race, **gender**, age, disability, religion, **class**, or ethnicity.

When you judge someone based on their ethnicity, you have made **assumptions** about that person based on rumors or stories about their culture and heritage. Sometimes people judge others based on their class. This means that they judge others based on how rich or poor they are and how popular they are in their community. To stop prejudice, people have to remind themselves to stop making unfair assumptions.

What Is Discrimination?

Discrimination is an act of racism or prejudice. Racism is the thought, and discrimination is when a person acts on these racist thoughts. Discrimination is unjust treatment of someone because of who they are. Calling someone a name because of his or her religion or refusing to treat a person with **equality** because of his or her race are both examples of discrimination.

What Is Privilege?

In the past, racism and prejudice were often easy to identify. Today, these behaviors can be much more **subtle** or hidden. For example, some people have more rights or advantages because of their ethnicity, gender, class, or sexual orientation. This is called privilege. The people benefitting from this privilege often do not recognize it. It may seem so natural in fact, that they deny it it even exists. Privilege means that some people are given **preferential** treatment in restaurants and stores. They may be hired over others for certain jobs, not because they deserve it or worked hard for it, but because they have always been entitled to it. Privilege can also mean freedom from fear that you will be a target of discrimination.

Privilege gives some people unearned perks.

"We don't talk too much about race but it is
everywhere. You can't avoid it. I think people are
afraid of what they might say if pushed and that
means they are afraid of showing their true colors.
I don't know if that's good or not. "
Avery, aged 17.

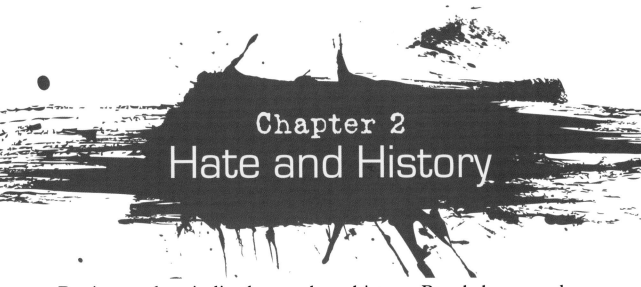

Chapter 2
Hate and History

Racism and prejudice have a long history. People have used racism and prejudice to tear down, hurt, and dehumanize others for hundreds of years. Dehumanization is what happens when one group attempts to make another seem less human, and therefore not equal or worthy of respect. Everyone has a role to play in ending racism and prejudice, but racism and prejudice are also often **systemic**, and are reflected in all of a society's institutions, such as government, schools, and businesses. This means that ending racism and prejudice goes beyond personal or individual action.

Race and Slavery

Issues of race are controversial subjects today because of the history of slavery. For 400 years, black Africans were taken from their homes in Africa and forced by white Europeans into slavery in **colonies** throughout the **New World**. At the time, most white people justified slavery by claiming black people were not fully human. Even when the slave trade ended, the condition of slavery itself continued in Canada until 1834, and in the United States until 1865.

Legacy of Slavery

One of the **legacies** of slavery is 400 years of **stereotypes,** prejudice, and race hatred. Racism was used to **reinforce** slavery. If slaves were seen as less than human, then slave owners could claim they were not doing anything wrong in enslaving them. Stereotypes about slaves strengthened these opinions. Slaves were viewed as lazy and not hard working. Yet the unpaid labor of slaves helped build the economies of many countries in Europe, as well as North and South America. Racist stereotypes continued to exist because they served a purpose—to keep power and control in the hands of the slave owners. Today, many people avoid discussing slavery when they talk about racism because it is considered a shameful part of the past. Slavery may be over, but the racism it reinforced still exists.

"My grandmother survived the Holocaust but lost her entire family except for one cousin. I believe I owe it to her and to others to fight hatred and **anti-semitism."**
Mala, aged 17.

Race Hate and Genocide

Racism isn't simple. It is complicated and dangerous because it leads to horrible acts of hate. One of the ultimate expressions of racism is genocide, which is the deliberate killing of a large group of people of a specific race or ethnic group. Millions of people were killed during the slave trade. The Holocaust, during World War II, is one of the most frightening and well-known recent examples of genocide. During the Holocaust (1941-1945), the **Nazis** from Germany killed six million European Jews and other people because they believed they were racially inferior and undesirable. This highly organized genocide was a result of race hatred. It was state-sponsored, meaning that the government of Nazi Germany **persecuted** and murdered millions of people as part of a racist plan to rid Europe of all Jews and other people it detested.

Never Again

Many survivors of the Holocaust said "never again" would they allow this kind of mass hatred and killing to happen. Sadly, our world is full of racism and hate, and although we have made great changes in the last century, it is difficult to convince some people that racism and race hate is wrong. Many genocides happened before the Holocaust and several have happened since.

The Nazis killed millions in concentration camps.

Overt vs. Covert Racism

Slavery and genocide are obvious, or overt, examples of racism. When we think of racism we often think of these clear acts of violence or hatred. Overt acts of racism are actions that are clearly demonstrated and cannot be denied. Many racist acts today are covert, or hidden. Usually, covert acts of racism are denied or even justified as right by those committing them.

People are sometimes unaware that they are participating in covert racism. Imagine you are walking down the street in the middle of the day. You turn the corner and see another kid you don't know who is about your age walking toward you. The other kid is about your size and is dressed just like you. The only difference is that this kid has a different color of skin. Even though the kid is not doing anything to you, you make the decision to cross the street so you do not have to walk past him. Is this decision a racist one? If the reason for crossing the street was based on a **preconceived** notion—such as a belief that people of his ethnicity are more likely to hurt you, then yes, it was racist. Unreasonable fear of a person based on their skin color is prejudice.

Covert racism prevents us from really seeing and understanding people.

16

What's in a Name?

Another example of covert racism can be found in professional sports. Many sports teams have a name or a mascot taken from Native American culture. The Kansas City Chiefs, Atlanta Braves, Cleveland Indians, and Washington Redskins are a few examples. These teams have been around for decades. At many of these games fans chant stereotypical cheers that misrepresent Native American culture.

When fans are asked about Native American culture being made fun of in sports, most of the time you hear them exclaim, "It's only a sport!" or "Who cares? Just because we paint our faces like Indians and chant like them does not mean we are racist! We are having fun!" But is making fun of another culture

and calling it team spirit fun, or is it something more? At first glance they just seem like ordinary mascots with painted faces and funny war cries. If we take a closer look, we see something else. We see people who do not belong to that culture enjoying maintaining a stereotype and portraying a group of very diverse people as **caricatures**, or exaggerated jokes.

Stereotypes and jokey images misrepresent Native Americans.

17

Race and Science

There have been many attempts to justify racism and prejudice with science. All of them have tried to set up a **hierarchy** of racial superiority, where people of lighter skin are ranked above those with darker skin. In the 1800s, doctors measured heads and skulls claiming they could tell how smart a person of a specific race was by the size of their skulls. Some scientists tried to classify races into "civilized" and "savage," with the model for civilized being white and the model for savage being Native North American or African. Other scientists developed programs to improve the population by controlling who could have children. These programs, called eugenics, applied to people of color and others, such as the poor and those who had mental or physical disabilities. Even today, some scientists look for biological proof of race and intelligence, and race and crime, even though others have proven these things have no connection.

Phrenologists used models that mapped parts of the brain to determine character and ability.

Hatred Justified

Prejudice and hatred is not just aimed at people of different skin color or ethnic groups. Today, it is often seen as acceptable to be prejudiced against people of different religions, sexual orientations, abilities, class, and even size. Since prejudice is irrational, or not reasonable, people often justify their hatred. They may say that they don't hate gay people, but they just don't think they should have the right to "flaunt" or show their **homosexuality**. This assumes that **heterosexuality** is normal and homosexuality is abnormal, and only people of "normal" sexuality have the right to hold hands in public. In reality, both are normal. Heterosexuality may be more common and, because of this, less feared.

Like racism, prejudice is a harmful behavior that assigns certain privileges and rights to some people while removing them from others. Why should homosexual people holding hands be offensive to some people when heterosexual people holding hands is okay?

Some people think it is okay to hate and discriminate against gay people.

Hate is harmful. Studies have shown that dealing with discrimination and oppression can make people sick and lead to heart disease and mental disorders.

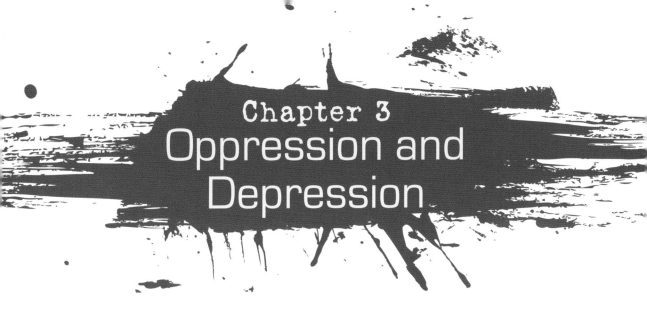

Chapter 3
Oppression and Depression

Racism and prejudice are oppressive. This means that both are unjustly harsh and cruel, and are used to try to control or have power over others. Quite often, people who are discriminated against are deprived of opportunities. Rather than being given all the tools they need to succeed, they are told or taught to believe that they do not deserve success, or that they have less potential than others. This is devastating not only for individuals, but for families, communities, and entire cultures. This cycle of **oppression** and **depression** spans generations, because it takes more than goodwill and anti-discrimination laws to change things.

Downpressors

Racism and prejudice are destructive forces. They take a toll on the oppressed and the oppressors alike. Racism informs values, and shapes opinions across society. It is not so easy to change racist ideals if people do not realize or accept that their actions are racist.

Fact and Fiction

Young people play a very important part in the elimination of racism and prejudice, but they are faced with many challenges. When we are young, we are taught to believe that authority figures are always right and that they must be respected. The truth is sometimes adults are misinformed. Remember, people are not born racist or prejudiced, but develop these thoughts and beliefs throughout their lifetimes because they were taught that one race is superior to another.

Imagine that a coach told you that you should try out for basketball and not golf because of your skin color or ethnicity. Would you listen to them? If a teacher told you that you should be on the math team and not in the drama club based on your race, would you take their advice? It may seem that these authority figures have your best interest in mind. After all, they are only trying to help you succeed, right? The problem is, their advice may be based on stereotypes and racist beliefs, and their suggestions may only hold you back.

Even supposedly good stereotypes, such as "all Asians are studious," are insulting and limiting.

Generalizations

Sometimes people think that certain races or cultures are better at specific sports or activities for scientific reasons. This is simply not true. No one race is biologically faster or smarter than another. Some individuals may be better at things because of opportunity. You can be sure that any time a person assumes one race is better than another at something, their assumptions are wrong. How do these stereotypes develop? If even adults believe them to be true, how can they be false? Stereotypes are generalizations about a certain group of people based on assumptions—not truths.

Stereotypes also exist outside of race and ethnicity. Some people stereotype gender, class, and sexual orientation. Making judgments based on assumptions leads to discrimination. It is important to realize that even if you think that your perception of a group of people is a positive one, you are still passing judgment on them.

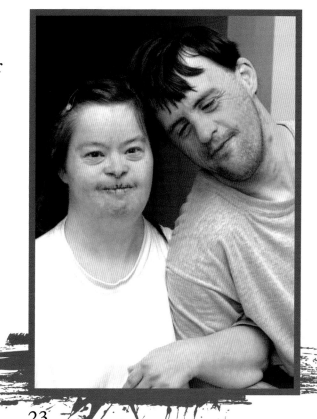

Making fun of people with physical and intellectual disabilities dehumanizes them and makes being hurtful seem okay.

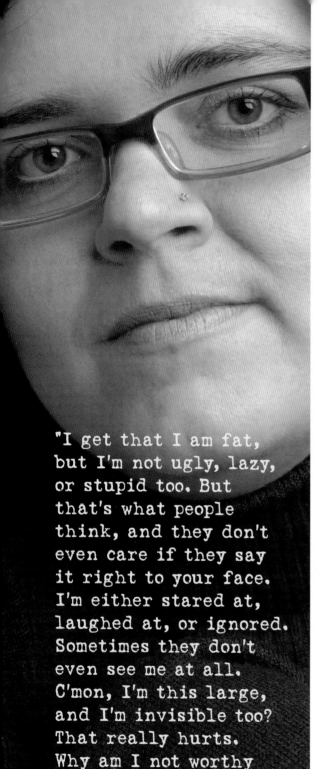

"I get that I am fat, but I'm not ugly, lazy, or stupid too. But that's what people think, and they don't even care if they say it right to your face. I'm either stared at, laughed at, or ignored. Sometimes they don't even see me at all. C'mon, I'm this large, and I'm invisible too? That really hurts. Why am I not worthy of respect just because I am a big girl?"
Juanita, aged 18.

Cultural Identity

It is not the case that one race or culture is better at a sport or an activity, but they may have had more exposure to it. They may have grown up in a town or neighborhood where that activity is more popular. When this is the case, the activity becomes a part of what is called cultural identity. Cultural identity is part of what forms the way a group sees themselves.

Some people's cultural identity includes their race or ethnicity, the place they grew up, and their hobbies and interests. Cultural identity can be a positive thing when it helps a person feel like they belong. It can be a great source of pride for a person and their community. Knowing your history and who you are can build self-esteem, which is important when dealing with prejudice.

24

Racism and Prejudice Hurt

The effects of racism are broad and deep and can harm individuals, families, and communities for years. Experiencing racism and prejudice is **traumatic**. Whether it is one single act or a lifetime of indignity and oppression, racism and prejudice can leave people feeling angry, humiliated, hurt, frustrated, and sad. Some people experience severe anxiety and depression because of the racism and prejudice they have suffered. They may even feel that the pain from taunts of hatred will never end, and suicide is the only option.

Racism can especially affect behavior when experienced in adolescence because it changes the way young people feel about themselves and the world around them. Racism and prejudice erode self-esteem, making it that much harder for people to believe they are capable, worthy, and important human beings. If you are constantly being told that you are not good enough because of who you are, you may begin to believe it. It takes a lot of courage and self-esteem to fight racism and prejudice

When open resistance to racism isn't possible, people use **passive resistance**, which requires a lot of control and feelings of self-worth.

"It's hard to trust people who are not my race or culture because I never know whether they will betray me or not."
Lisa, aged 15.

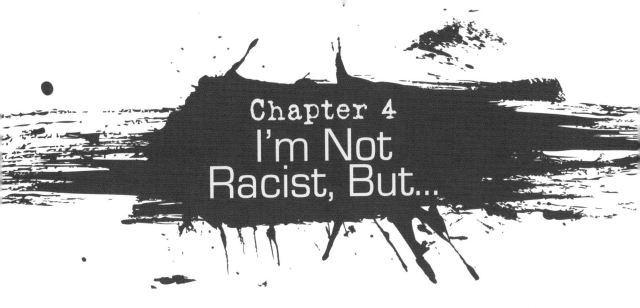

Chapter 4
I'm Not Racist, But...

Many decades ago, it was not only acceptable but legal to **segregate** people based on the color of their skin or their ehtnicity. Today, this type of discrimination is punishable by law, but often the segregation and prejudice remains. How is it possible that racist thoughts and beliefs still fill our world? It takes **resilience** for victims of racism and prejudice to fight off constant attacks and keep their sense of worth. Racist thoughts and behaviors must also consciously be "unlearned" by those who perpetrate them. This means accepting that your actions, including jokes, and the belief in stereotypes are wrong and must be changed. People often claim that they are not racist or prejudiced, but their actions betray their words.

Racism and prejudice are devastating. It's not just the obvious acts, such as name-calling or bullying, that hurt.

Justifying Hatred

Sometimes people justify their prejudices with excuses. They may claim they are not prejudiced but just dislike certain religions and the people who follow them. Or they may say things like, "I don't hate gay people, I just think what they do is wrong." It is like saying they do not hate not African Americans, but they just don't like black skin. The prejudice is still present. The assumption is that their values and **morals** are superior to someone else's. Justifying hatred often makes prejudice more socially acceptable and encourages others to act in hateful ways.

Teaching, Learning

Every year, you spend about 1,500 hours glued to your television set. While you learn a lot at school, you also learn a lot from television. You absorb ideas about race from the media. Some television shows portray the bad guy as one race and the hero as another. When was the last time you watched a movie or a television show where the lead character was Native American, gay, overweight, or disabled? Minorities are often **under-represented** or misrepresented in the media. This is a problem because certain races are continuously shown in a negative way or are not shown at all. Are these types of people not worth the viewer's time? Are they less entertaining or interesting? If we are shown the same types of prejudices often enough, we may begin to see them as the truth.

NO RACISM

The Many Faces of Racism

Racism has many faces and takes many forms. Racism can be a thought. It can be an offhand comment or a deliberate action. Racism can also be the absence of action. When you know that something wrong is happening, sitting back and doing nothing is just as destructive as the act of discriminating. People need to learn how to identify racism, stop it in action, and even try to prevent it from occurring.

Racism also has many colors, shapes, and sizes. Even people from groups that are discriminated against can be racist and prejudiced. Racism prevents people from seeing other individuals as human beings.

We need to be aware that stereotypes exist for all cultures, ethnicities, and abilities.

Talking About It

Everyone has been exposed to stereotypes and racism. A big part of unlearning prejudiced thoughts is to talk about them. Talking to our friends and family, guidance counselors, coaches, and teachers about racism and prejudice makes it easier to identify and learn about these issues. Talking about racism can also help with fear and coping with its effects. Racism and prejudice have a devastating effect on people. Over time, they can make people feel like they are worthless. Psychologists call this internalizing because victims absorb the hate directed toward them and use it to devalue themselves and sometimes others, as well.

Words Have Meaning

People use hurtful language and terms every day, often without even thinking about what they are saying. Some people use language to make them feel part of a group. Words like "cool" and "awesome" are used to describe things they like. Sometimes, people use inappropriate words to describe things they do not like. How many times have you heard friends describe something they dislike as "gay," "lame," or "retarded"? These words are not innocent jokes. They have powerful meanings. Used this way, language is a tool for isolating and degrading people based on their sexual orientation and physical and mental abilities.

Am I Racist or Prejudiced?

Most people don't want to be considered racist or prejudiced. They like to think they are good and fair to everyone, no matter their sex, gender, ethnicity, or ability. However, people often show who they are through their actions. Are you racist or prejudiced? Could you do some work to improve how you treat people? Read and answer the questions below:

Do you routinely make friends only with people from your own ethnic group. If so, ask yourself why. Is it because you don't know anyone from another culture or because you don't associate with people from other groups?

Do you laugh at racist or sexist jokes when someone tells them? Do you really think they are funny?

Do you treat schoolmates with disabilities differently? Why?

Do you make judgements about people because of how they dress. For example, do you automatically think all senior citizens are forgetful or that poor people are less sophisticated?

Do you think people with lighter skin color are smarter than people with darker skin color?

Do you think people who are overweight are also lazy?

Do you think some religions are "wrong" and yours is "right"?

Would you go out with or date someone from a different ethnic group or religion?

31

"It's not just the jokes, it's the outrageous things people say and get away with because people pick their battles. I'm talking ordinary people who say things like 'dreads are filthy' or 'he really jewed-me down'. Seriously? You can't check your language? Some people can't be shamed."
Alicia, adult anti-racism activist.

Chapter 5
No Laughing Matter

You've probably heard racist, sexist, or **homophobic** jokes in the schoolyard or on the street. You might have been tempted to chuckle at them or repeat them. People often think that jokes that make fun of someone's race, sex, or religion are completely harmless. But they are usually the ones telling the jokes and not the ones being laughed at. Making a joke about an entire group of people is hurtful and reinforces stereotypes and prejudices. These jokes aren't funny. They are mean.

So, how do you deal with racist jokes? When people make racist jokes or comments, it may not be the best use of your time to give them a lecture on racism and discrimination. The most effective thing to do is let them know that what they are saying is not funny. Of course, this is easier to do if the joke isn't about you. People who make these types of comments are looking for a laugh. They want to be liked by their peers and often make jokes at another person's expense in order to appear funny or cool. Is that the type of person you want to be? Is it the type of person you want to hang out with?

Sticks and Stones

The Internet has opened up a new world of communication. It is being used to educate, inform, and update on all kinds of topics. Unfortunately, the Internet can be used for evil, as well. Many people have used it as a tool to spread messages of hate and prejudice all over the world. Groups and individuals that spread these types of messages are sometimes called extremists. They spread lies about ethnic groups and their opinions go unchallenged.

"I don't know what's worse, the people who hate me because I am Native American or those who want to tell me about my history because I'm too ignorant and deprived to know it. Believe me, I know who I am. I live it every day."
Bryce, aged 18.

You can't believe everything you read on the Internet.

Hate Crimes

What happens when the hate goes beyond jokes and comments? What if someone acts on their racist thoughts or beliefs? When a person commits a crime against another person because of a protected characteristic it is called a hate crime. A protected characteristic may include race, gender, sexual orientation, gender identity, religion, disability, ethnicity, or nationality. While laws surrounding hate vary from state to state in the United States, current laws allow all hate crimes to be federally prosecuted. This means that instead of going to trial at the state level, a person charged with a hate crime could face a federal trial. Some people consider hate crimes to be worse than other types of crimes because the offender is specifically targeting their victim based on prejudices. This means that a hate crime not only devastates the victim's family and friends, but also all those who identify with the victim.

Hate groups often blame their problems on people of other races. They are often accused of encouraging hate crimes.

"Small acts of resistance and solidarity can help
tear down walls and build understanding just as
much as these larger acts. You don't have an anti-
racist concert or event every day, but you can make
little changes that have a great impact on people
around you each day."
Efia, foreign exchange student.

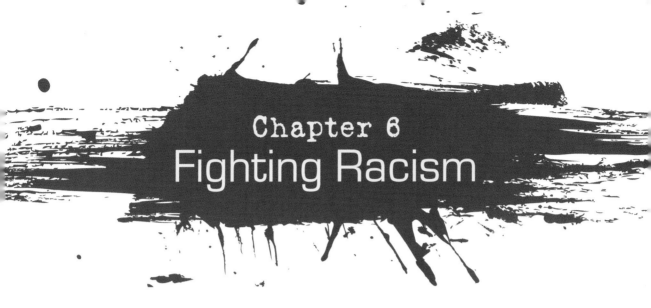

Chapter 6
Fighting Racism

Racism and prejudice can be difficult to hear about and hard to understand. Hatred is hurtful and can destroy people's sense of self and community. The impact of racism and prejudice is wide. Victims feel frightened. Their friends and families may feel scared and angry, as well.

But there are things that we can do to limit and stop racism and prejudice. We can voice our disapproval with its ideas and help create a safer and more peaceful environment for everyone. The actions and steps we can take are sometimes small, but impressive. You do not have to stage rallies and protests to stop racism and prejudice. You can be involved in stopping racism and prejudice simply by acknowledging they exist and resisting them. Resistance can take on many forms, such as celebrating diversity in your classroom and inviting people to share their culture and experiences, to questioning racist comments. You can also educate yourself about what is going on in your community and world and read books written by people of different ethnic or religious backgrounds.

"How do you stand up and say something when you are afraid?"
Zabel, aged 14.

What Comes Next?

When we see racism and prejudice happen to others, it can be a scary moment. You may feel many emotions such as fear, surprise, shock, or horror. If you are the target of hateful words or actions, it will be even more upsetting. But what happens after the words are said and everybody leaves? The impact of these words affects people in a variety of different ways. Sometimes people will become withdrawn and quiet. They may try to keep their heads down so no one else will call them a hurtful name. Others may deal with the hurt by becoming angry. They may start to lash out at people who stood by and did nothing, or even at people who are close to them.

Resisting Racism and Prejudice

Fighting racism and prejudice can seem like an enormous responsibility. Opposition toward racism can start with just one person doing what is right. You do not need a big group of people or money. Here are some easy actions you can take to help fight racism:

Speak up against racism and prejudice when you see it happening. Speak out when you hear racial slurs, or insults, or prejudiced comments. If you do not feel safe speaking up, find a friend or adult you trust and discuss what you witnessed.

Learn about different cultures. Check out your local library or community center for upcoming festivals, film screenings, or celebrations hosted by different cultural communities.

Start an anti-racism group in your school or community. Find a teacher or other adult to give you support and recruit your friends and classmates to join in. If you cannot start a group, check your school or library to see if they already have a group that works toward ending prejudice.

Take a good look around your community. Racism and prejudice happen in every corner of the world, including your own. Talk about racism and prejudice with your friends. If you have used racial slurs or called people names in the past, recognize that this is wrong. If you can, try to apologize to those you have hurt.

Hear other people's stories. Listen, have compassion, and support what they share with you. When you listen to the experiences of others you strengthen your own decision to fight racism and prejudice.

Seeking Help

It is not easy to deal with things alone. Being the victim of racist or prejudiced acts can be overwhelming. You may be afraid of what might happen to you or stressed from trying to control your impulse to lash out. You may want to turn to a friend or family member for support and advice. Just remember that speaking up about your experiences won't make them go away, but there is comfort in numbers—in knowing that others have had similar experiences and can tell you how they dealt with them.

Helping a Friend

When a friend comes to you for help, listen to them. When you actively listen to your friend you are not just listening—you are letting your friend know that what they are saying

is important and that you are hearing them. Support your friend in what they want to do and believe what they are saying. Sometimes it can feel like a very big job to help someone who has been hurt by racist actions, and you may need the support of a trusted adult.

Be a good friend by supporting and listening without judgment.

Suffering the Effects

Sometimes people who have experienced acts of racism and prejudice have difficulty dealing with the pain and trauma. They may suffer low self-esteem, depression, anxiety, and post-traumatic stress disorder (PTSD) as a result. Severe anxiety can make it difficult to live a normal life, as people may have frequent panic attacks that make it difficult to face the outside world. People who are depressed may have difficulty concentrating and may feel sad and worthless a lot of the time. PTSD is a disorder brought on by traumatic events. People with PTSD often re-experience traumatic events. They do not just remember, but truly feel as though they are back in time reliving the experience that traumatized them. They can also experience flashbacks, nightmares and night terrors, difficulty sleeping, and feel angry and irritated.

Joining a club or keeping physically active playing sports, running, or walking can help you deal with the stress and anxiety of racism and prejudice.

Chapter 7
Coping Toolbox

Keeping yourself and those around you safe from the hurtful effects of racism and prejudice is important. You may find you already have a lot of what psychologists call coping mechanisms. These are things you do to deal with the stress and upset. Healthy coping behaviors include talking about your feelings with a close friend or relative, writing your thoughts down in a journal, or exercising to get your frustrations out in a way that does not hurt you or other people.

Staying Safe

Racism and prejudice can have both immediate and long-term effects on a person. The immediate effects can include feeling fearful, angry, and hurt. The long-term effects can include loss of self-esteem, anxiety, and depression. It is okay to feel emotional when you are a victim of prejudice. You have been unjustly harmed, and it is important to remember that it is not your fault.

Coping Tips

Racism and prejudice can be so harmful that they destroy a person's sense of safety, and confidence in their own worth. It might be helpful to make a list of ways to deal with racism and prejudice so you can keep your self-esteem intact.

If someone is threatening you and your safety is an immediate concern, look for assistance. Call friends, police, or a hotline. Do what you can to avoid racist abuse.

Talk about the act of racism or prejudice with a trusted friend, relative, teacher, minister, or counselor.

Write your feelings down in a notebook or journal. Writing may help you understand what happened.

Act out your frustrations in a role playing exercise with friends. It helps to do this when you are calm. Try saying what you really want to say to those who have hurt you—without anger and name-calling.

Learn how to assert yourself. It is not easy to speak up during a situation, and sometimes it is not possible. Practice speaking your mind in a non-confrontational manner. It may be difficult to do this at first.

Avoid taking your anger and frustration out on yourself, your friends, or your family. Do not turn to alcohol or drugs to dull the pain. Drugs or alcohol may temporarily numb your feelings, but they will always come back.

Racism and prejudice is aimed at making you feel bad about yourself. Do not give anyone the power to destroy your faith in yourself.

Join an organization that fights for human rights and equality.

Hot Topics
Q&A

Q: Why can't I use racist words in a friendly way? I hear people using them all the time with their friends and family. If they can use these words, why am I not allowed to?

A: Some people try to reclaim racist words in an effort to make those words less powerful and less hurtful. They may use the words in an attempt to make their meaning more positive, instead of a hurtful reminder of racism. But words having meaning and racist slurs are very offensive to many people. Try to connect in a different way.

Q: My dad talks about our neighbors all the time. He says that they are lazy and should "go back to where they came from." This makes me feel bad. What should I do?

A: It is always difficult to hear adults, especially ones we love and respect, say hurtful and racist things. You can choose a moment where your dad is not talking about the neighbors and let him know that you feel uncomfortable when he says these things. You may not be able to change his opinion, but letting him know that you are not interested in hearing this is important.

Q: I called someone a racist name in school. I know it was wrong and feel bad about it. What can I do to reverse the hurt I caused?

A: The first thing to do is to recognize that you made a mistake. The next step is to admit to the person you hurt that it was wrong. Do not tell them you were only joking and do not expect them to make you feel better. Offer an apology and change your behavior.

Q: Am I prejudiced if I think it is weird that a kid in my class has gay parents?

A: It's not weird to have gay parents. It is different from what you are used to and that may be why you think it is weird. Sometimes things, people, or situations that are different can make people fearful or uncomfortable. You are judging your classmate's family as weird without knowing anything about them, which is one of the definitions of prejudice.

Q: There is a group of kids at school who make fun of one student because he is Hispanic. They used to make fun of me because of my weight, but now they tease him instead. I want them to stop but I am also afraid they will attack me again. What should I do?

A: Remember what it was like when you were teased? Did you wish that someone had stepped in to support you? No one likes to be teased, and when teasing happens because of race or weight, it is especially hurtful. If you are not feeling safe confronting the bullies in your school, you may want to approach your teacher or an adult you trust. As well, you may want to think about talking to the student being teased. Let your classmate know that he or she is not alone and you are supporting them.

Other Resources

Racism and prejudice are complex issues. It is almost impossible to go through life without witnessing an act of hate, hearing a racist comment, or experiencing prejudice. The more we are exposed to these types of things, the more questions we may find ourselves asking. Here is a list of trustworthy resources to help you. The Web sites will contain useful information no matter which country you live in, but telephone numbers and referral services will be country-specific.

In the United States
NAACP

www.naacp.org
The official site of the National Association for the Advancement of Colored People, an organization that has been working to eliminate racial hatred and discrimination since 1909. The site provides information on NAACP programs, youth initiatives, research, and advocacy.

Youth Resource

www.amplifyyourvoice.org/youthresource
YouthResource is a Web site by and for gay, lesbian, bisexual, transgender, and questioning youth. It answers questions and concerns, and provides support to those in need.

Boys Town National Hotline
1-800-448-3000
This crisis line is for adolescents, teens, and parents who need help with any problem. The counseling service is free of charge and available 24-hours-a-day, seven-days-a-week.

GLBT National Youth Talkline
1-800-246-PRIDE (1-800-246-7743)
This hotline offers telephone peer counseling to gay, lesbian, bisexual, transgendered, and questioning youth, Monday to Friday from 5-9 p.m. (Pacific Time).

In Canada
What's the Deal?
www.deal.org
This s a great Web site aimed at young people who want to put an end to hate. Check out articles on how to navigate bias in your community and blogs on bullying and racism.

Artists Against Racism
www.artistsagainstracism.org
This site has great anti-racism television commercials, print advertisements, and radio stations that you can check out. There are up-to-date articles in the news section that will keep you in the know. Browse the list of celebrities involved, and click the "Get Involved" link for great advice!

Kids Help Phone
1-800-668-6868
www.kidshelpphone.ca
This is a Canadian-only crisis line. Professional counselors can answer any questions and give you referrals to services in your area.

Glossary

anti-semitism Hostility or prejudice against Jews

assumptions Something accepted as truth without proof

biologically From nature or our anatomy

caricatures Exaggerated pictures often created for humor

class Economic status in society

colonies Areas or countries under the control of another country and occupied by settlers

cultural Relating to the ideas and customs of a society

depression A mental disorder or condition marked by feelings of hopelessness

discrimination Unjust treatment of people

ethnic Relating to a group of people with a common cultural tradition

equality The same in rights, opportunity, and status

gender The social characteristics or roles associated with being male or female

genetically Relating to heredity or origin

hate crimes Crimes committed against a person or group based on extreme prejudice

heterosexuality Attracted to the opposite sex

hierarchy A classification of people by rank or class

hijab The head covering and modest style of dress traditionally worn by Muslim women

homophobic Irrational dislike for homosexual people

homosexuality Attracted to the same sex

legacies Something handed down from the past

morals Concerned with wrong and right

Nazis People who belonged to a racist political party that ruled Germany from 1933 to 1945

New World North and South America

offensive Causing someone to feel very hurt, or angry

oppression Unjust or cruel control

passive resistance Nonviolent opposition to authority or systemic racism

persecuted Hostile treatment of a person or group based on their race or beliefs

preconcieved An opinion formed before having the facts

preferential Giving privilege or advantage

reinforce Strengthen

resilience Able to withstand and recover

segregate Divided according to race

sexual orientation The sex a person is attracted to

stereotypes Widely held but oversimplified views or images of someone or something

subtle So slight or precise it is difficult to see

superficial Not thorough or deep

superior Higher in rank or more important

systemic Throughout society

tolerates To accept or endure something that that you don't necessarily agree with

traumatic Emotionally distressing

unbiased Showing no prejudice

underrepresented Not represented the way something should be

Index